T0125966

THE
MIRRORMAKER

ALSO BY BRIAN LAIDLAW

The Stuntman

THE
MIRRORMAKER

POEMS

BRIAN LAIDLAW

MILKWEED EDITIONS

© 2018, Text by Brian Laidlaw

All rights reserved. Except for brief quotations in critical articles or reviews, no part of this book may be reproduced in any manner without prior written permission from the publisher: Milkweed Editions, 1011 Washington Avenue South, Suite 300, Minneapolis, Minnesota 55415.

(800) 520-6455

milkweed.org

Published 2018 by Milkweed Editions
Printed in the United States
Cover design by Mary Austin Speaker
Cover photo by Chris Morgan
Author photo by Colin Copp
18 19 20 21 22 5 4 3 2 1
First Edition

Milkweed Editions, an independent nonprofit publisher, gratefully acknowledges sustaining support from the Jerome Foundation; the Lindquist & Vennum Foundation; the McKnight Foundation; the National Endowment for the Arts; the Target Foundation; and other generous contributions from foundations, corporations, and individuals. Also, this activity is made possible by the voters of Minnesota through a Minnesota State Arts Board Operating Support grant, thanks to a legislative appropriation from the arts and cultural heritage fund, and a grant from Wells Fargo. For a full listing of Milkweed Editions supporters, please visit milkweed.org.

Library of Congress Cataloging-in-Publication Data

Names: Laidlaw, Brian, 1983- author.
Title: The mirrormaker : poems / Brian Laidlaw.
Description: First edition. | Minneapolis, Minnesota : Milkweed Editions, 2018.
Identifiers: LCCN 2018013310 (print) | LCCN 2018033568 (ebook) | ISBN 9781571319487 (ebook) | ISBN 9781571314840 (pbk. : alk. paper)
Classification: LCC PS3612.A397 (ebook) | LCC PS3612.A397 A6 2018 (print) | DDC 811/.6--dc23
LC record available at https://lccn.loc.gov/2018013310

Milkweed Editions is committed to ecological stewardship. We strive to align our book production practices with this principle, and to reduce the impact of our operations in the environment. We are a member of the Green Press Initiative, a nonprofit coalition of publishers, manufacturers, and authors working to protect the world's endangered forests and conserve natural resources. *The Mirrormaker* was printed on acid-free 30% postconsumer-waste paper by Versa Press.

To Ash

CONTENTS

I.

II.

III.

Epilogue

Acknowledgments

Liner Notes

He didn't talk to me—he talked into a mirror—I did not have
the courage to crash or shatter myself.

BOB DYLAN
Tarantula

I.

Echo's Ailments

to call something *harmless* admits
a certain potential

for harm (*love* is not & neither
is *unknowing*)—

homes on dead-flats
sink into prairie sinks; gradations

from *landslide* to *landfall*

to *rock-fall* to *rockabilly* to *rock-a-bye*

bifurcate the county—
we watch half a mountain collapse

like a stroked face, then we

help the half that didn't
collapse collapse

Hatches

tallnorthcountrygirl is the tallest
landmark

man looks up her skirt
madams too whistling

downtown
(she necessitates downtown)—I would like your eye

level, I would like a haystack to climb
your effervescence

tallnorthcountrygirl thrills
the bees of the brush

I love you so much I want you

to walk in a trench wheresoever
you walk

beside me
here

I'll dig it

Iron Ironworker

the world's largest handwritten promise, the world's largesse

the largest choir of mouthless, of eyeless,
of coins in their eyes & mouths

the pale ground-dwellers sport
the world's largest malfunctioning optic nerve

the world's largest hollow red balloon
imitating a crater

made by the largest volcano the world's ever imagined,
the world's overlarge largesse

the world's largest open pit
sore, the open mine shutting the world's largest sunroof

the largest fall rollover ever viewed from the world's largest
desk, the largest sun, & the darkest,

& the darkness that siphons the world's largest sunroom

Twin Brothers Drowning in a Flooded Ore Pit

There were cliffs to get knocked unconscious stepping from, walls
a dinghy dashes apart against,
many-a-boy's aqueous grave, the burdens

stirring below, a knot of metals
impressive as the world's largest iron sculpture of a man sculpting iron.
Your bodies choke on behalf of your lungs, your hands are oars, dumbly, such
castoffs, such postconsumer finitude
in the pit ponds,
a cupid punchout astern—

I can't tell if utility is always mutual (*It isn't*)
I wish I were fine in layoffs (*You're never*)
I think the shit of life settles out, the slick thermoclines—

I think hierarchy is romantic—
you become it, it becomes you.

The Sparrows

the sparrows dirty
the windows

with red
spreadeagle sparrow prints

they take turns committing
pretend suicides

striking the kite paper morning

like typewriter mallets
all Xs

they dance a dance
called *formerness*

Echo is them

Medicine Cabinet Inventory

the cigar man & the cigar box is one
the cigar man & the box & the boxcar

is one
the box guitar & the vox & the voice box &
the talkie is one

    the echo is another

the coda in the corner the doorman the coatman
the eyeless fox &

his eyelets is one
the honey leaf cigar & the honey leaf
& the honey is one &

    the echo is another

The Dinosaurs

//

the dinosaurs died

in a red cloud the kids learnt

in our good schools

our world class

approaches

I like to watch a hill unfurl to me

like a woman wearing a flag for a dress

this I like to happen

at all tempos—I am not hasty

I am not like a halogen light or a hydrogen bomb

& I am not crude like oil—

I am refined like oil

//

our good school's children

came from monkeys

the dolomitic white earth is white with

dinosaur bone—is red with red remnants

of hominid blood

(never forget)

our offspring should live without withholding

(the key to the kingdom)

& without holding back—

a piano in every parlour,

touring divas, the nation's deepest pool—the earth itself

is unworthy of our children's love

Echo's Impressions

//

Echo does impressions: bombs for pom-poms, bombshells for kneepads,
knee-deep in your/man's notions of *feasible*

//

Nobody going nowhere fast. You got licked by a greyhound
station, licked clear cold out

It was similar to having or to
being a mother:

here's to being heretofore human, here's
to the time being.

//

You, swimming in moons, machinery, liquids, assets, have a voice

like a strangulation
victim, born out of the wrong end, out of a mouth like a slur.

//

I am a visual statement
of myself, while you

loom acoustic.

//

Echo is a sugarsweet gumshoe; chewing gum
drops your white teeth right out

You'll rap an oldtime rag on her behalf, you say "There's a shake shop
downtown with curlicue straws" &

she rephrases
"There's a maltshop downtown with a roundabout bar."

//

Also: the beautiful don't die young, only their beauty does.

Upstate Mothers

//

upstate mothers

were wont to laissez faire

boys ran rampant

on the lassies & borders

we torch dead elms

like ten elkhorns

a raring

oil in the boiler

like old faithfuls of

doric fire

//

I had a house on my shoulders

threw stones through

my own wind-

ows to get a rise

scratch & sniff turned into scratch & win

I bet on foolery

journey & jury as workforce

were a pair of clubs

in my hand

some would rail the rail-

ties down

as though they were jaws

& some broke jaws as though

they were errant

rail-ties

//

snow makes the globe grow

while making it look like it's shrinking

doesn't it mom

I cartograph the grant line

make a globe

shoot some bottle rockets at coppers

it makes me grow

it makes me look like I'm thinking

Playtime Empire

where the hell is my dollhouse
I accuse that you broke in

you or your special friend
threw my toy home into your golf cart—   *it is utilitarian but not useful*
                                            two matte jet trails from its fourwheels

dug a grave for the cutaway cabin & torched it
its subterranean chimney
ugly as a geranium—   *sickle petals billow out*
                                            of Echo's mouth

like refinery smoke—   *not at all*
                                            like bonfire smoke

all my resources pass through this burnt window, solar, sonar,
the napkin-sized curtains wilting everywhere—

                                            you took my house & put it in your yard

I know what you did to Tom Sawyer, to Tom Thumb, to Thumbelina—
condemned them to wanting

ever-bigger worlds

The Golden Rule of Copyright

the first time I saw the moon

I thought it was my own idea

damn plagiarists

I said—or I thought

I also thought I invented some heartstrings

that behave like bungees

& some other ones that behave like nooses

tugging that silver prototype back, &

back & forth

the idea of originality may

be the most unoriginal idea in history—

just ask Echo

we want to invent a microphone that makes the moon its coil

then we can worry

about our *phase relationships*

dear plagiarists

the moon is responsible for its own reinvention

& so is everyone else

Dark Sides

who knows what makes me

who knows

if that makes me anything

but I know

whether the moon winks

or coyly says o or O

a big dark

angel face is around it

& she's ambidextrous

& it's androgynous

& they like me

to be like them

I heard an alternate gospel

I shut my eyes & my teeth

II.

Echo's Theory

I still don't know   *Echo thinks she walks on air*
who I am   *thehypotheticalchild is born onto glass*

                            a vast glass shelf over a cavernous no

when it's dark the subject: *sees her footsoles*
when light: *she dapples the brush at a remove*

suspense becomes a theory of death

                    what is it to walk a glass plank
                    what happens to her when she reaches the edge of the glass
                    having only ever seen glass

here are footfalls; here our other baby shoe drops

the town has a tongue it let loll and lapse

the terrarium town over which this glass is is

equally mute

                    thehypotheticalchild plays hopscotch
                    there are diamond drill-bits on the soles of her shoes

if you love them cut out their floor

gouge the visibility of their beautiful eyes out

I met someone good   *she was like a window display of a town*
named after a vanishment
she twiddles her thumbs

the thesis not disproven   *she taps the town's glass baffles*

Father, you don't know what sustainable is
was Echo's first theory of her own

Holster, Upholster

you look like a historical reenactment of yourself
in a suburban parlor. history allows
but low tolerance for visual disarray; we visit a cold
war bungalow which

smells like elderly catwomen
the chapeau perches atop a soviet globe
honey reconnoiters & reconsiders who killed
your youthful *you*, who put your collectible

cereal spoons in a purple display. life has a silver lining but death's
is velvet, the room being
the room where Jesus seemed implausible
to a youngun

this is where the penis was discovered
this is where I learned where Canada was
these are original duplicates of the original wall hangings
this globe represents an earlier globe representing an earlier earth: look

at the redrawn Baltic the red redrawn guns on the icebox reefer
I suggest you get more interested in yourself
the attic, the Adriatic, you shipbound
parroting humanist lists

the chamfer edges of the mirror
the outdoors shut indoors
the field farther afield
the replica me heartbreaking the replica you

Dead Pony Recapitulation

//

you come in swinging fists resembling everybody,

     punching noses. your death could be in the rain & it wouldn't know

     a cross is a form of counterpoint,
     an annal across your chest
     feeling elective, feeling electric

I disbelieve in failure
the easiest person to threaten is yourself
buildings are impossible, camaraderie, every flag
     is at half mast twice a day on razing etc

nothing amounts to anything
     but *nothing* is a realm of infinite possibility

     like a carousel
     where all the ponies are unicorns
     coaxed into action

what is the kingdom like where everyone is a princess & am I there yet
what is adulthood like & why do I care so fucking little

I missed the day they said *think small*
I skipped the day they said *causality*
I missed a lot of days because I was sick or broken
I missed the causation day because . . .

//

are we there yet I slurred
we said some fables, grew out our leg hair

    to closer resemble tigers unsuccessfully & tigresses

the flag we salute is magnetic & the country's sad as a dead pony riding
into town on a shopping cart
are we there yet it slurs back
emerald city, motor city, engram city

if god's on a seesaw
across from me I don't
know who is the upside, & who
is the downside

Fractal

you tell me all day that body & mind are one

that slag & ore are of a piece

while everyday my shoulders attempt to crawl over my ears

like two dogs stalking a lamb

which is finally thought

paradise is panting

it has raspberry elbows

heaven & hell are in your mind you say

unity is abiding

fine

but if we are a completeness

then what is killing what

Chevron

Echo, powdering her nose with arsenic, tests the bouquet

of toxin in the watershed. How long
can one love a golem,

was all autumn a cesspool, a success, a love
into which she fell? To debrief:

the geese shat in the quarry, the quarry
was poison. The outlook was scenic.

The sick of the fields ran riverward.
I am going to grow

into something beautiful; there is an organism
that can only live in a goose's asshole,

life produces this elegance like Mother Mary:
Christ was inconceivable

(*honk honk says the chevron in the slagpile pond*)

but he was, regardless, conceived.

They Found a Wolf

they found a wolf

out on the town curb

with a bloated belly

I came to look

I thought it was pregnant

its young rustled inside

they cut the belly open

like a gourd & out burst

a green lotus

a many-petaled

ruffle of bills

the wolf has died from eating money

they said

& they laughed

Echo's Prom

Echo is hung like a poorly hung painting
Echo is hung like a poorly hung horse

Echo is *off the wall*
the mountains diminish

from D cup to B cup

the inverse prom
the inverse adolescence

a Sadie Hawkins
apocalypse Echo

invited me to
but I will pan on pretense through my empty

datebook—   *my book full of notes but no engagements*
                                       I think the constellations are made of metallic tears

                                       like salt in a punchbowl of black wine

              I said yes

but something disastrous can still smile on a man
fame is not ha-ha

funny
you have to bleed a ton of blood to get that red

but I'll come linger, window-shop—

we are the only high-school in the world
with a wrought-iron dance-floor

every student has an oil rendering of
him or herself

I'm collecting them for a city-size yearbook—note—
I'm not inviting you

to the afterparty,
I'm just inviting it to take place.

No Anemics

hold hands let's walk to the foundry

my body shows up in compasses

you can see it from space

the evidence of absence

visible from satellites

this American eagle dips

a metallic wing in

the town's undercarriage

visible from everywhere

stumbling into itself

there's no reflection

in that vat but

I show up in your x-ray visions

kissing the taconite

garret of your mouth

Anechoic

//

a seizure
is a possession & a repossession

I have demons but they needn't ride me

a prepossession

like a biplane splinted together

glacial body
avalanche body
onus body

like a rockslide
deaf looseness breaks me

they march
my skeleton up a real spiral stair

always barely old enough
to see how dumb & young I was

//

the valentine heartshape, it is established,
is nothing

like the heart
in design—it is much more like the blade of a shovel

           & similarly it kills with manners
           both quickly & slowly

//

lub dub is dug nearby
the town could use a rebirth but would settle for a reburial

the town's heartshape hull makes raking
sounds, it is intent

on being hellbent on being
settled—like its two stop signs, like its one

stoplight, the town knows
a tad bit about love

           & Echo is in it.

//

so hungry you don't know you're hungry
so rich you forget you're rich

I would like to die throat first
I would like a wolf

to eat my adam's apple, see my spine
through that red window

you held this head high some days
you would be right to die nodding

lucky dog, luckily nodding

//

I wear a bib out to the bar now
so I can nosebleed onto it

     I am awash   *I have no washerwoman*
                                 I am no washerwoman

prosperity songs
aren't worthless

                                 but they don't
                                 barter ore for them

you can't feed a dog a song to keep it from starving

                                 I have a fat fat dog
                                 & it knows its name

//

he devours my bloody bib
like a biography

he carries me dead
robins   *I love you*
                                                like a hellhound

                                                I love you
                                                like a dingo

//

in the hospital hall

I am a wreck & yet
I am reckless   *riddle me that*

the flower is an explosion
the flower flows upward

                                 like a pyrotechnic column

abrupt finale

                                 you too

are a missile of *self* shot
into a commons of *selfless*

//

gauze swaddling my palms
I worry

I am a bouquet of roses
blushing for pluckers   *they wore gloves*

    & conscience is a runaway fist

full of flowers
in reverse bloom   *violet eye,*
                                                         forget-me-not

//

I thought I saw Pegasus   *afar*
but it was a hawk
uplifting a fawn   *up close*

                    the ecosystem wants an eye for an eye
                    but the ecosystem has no eye

save the raptors
active within it

//

I bludgeon America
I have the necessary permits
the fawn said an aria   *close up*

the windpipe organ had music in it
a red outburst like the shift was ending   *afar*

the taproot is onto something

arterial blood,
red raw cream

//

you check your scansion & discover
you don't care

"the rose rose"

& fission & fusion is godliness   *by another name*

you don't care about modesty, being miracle

everything's equally rare, the kiss of death
is every kiss & every death

so they snub cigarettes out in the orchard

//

sometimes it's like the rooms are made
　　of hummingbirds &

　　　　I am in a vest of cassette
　　　　　　tapes' eviscera

　　　　　　Echo is a　tautology
　　　　　　you can't

　　　　say the same thing
　　　　　　twice over　ever

//

of that night I remember nothing
but the Polaroids

are full of love, the tiniest bluebird bows the tiniest violin
piecing the room's

beamy airspace
into discernible bits. it was beautiful onstage, blue snow of bluebirds

in auroras. this is not honest
but you can echolocate honesty

in the magnetic arc of it. my face is relaxed, I could be asleep.
electricity humming dumb.

//

heaven is a talent show;
hell is a talent show.

you look for the one
with amps & a good soundman

& an audience
more windows than mirrors;

you hope for some applause
to reveal what show you're in.

//

I sang properly.
that *sang* in French is *blood*

is a fact I know. curtains
nocked up in the corners as baffles

to mute echoes in the bandroom & douse
drafts dead out. when I concentrate

I can see bluebirds humming, hummingbird-sized around my temples
like I am headshot

& the blowback is an aviary—
if you hear the chirr & the whirr, if I am a stirrup,

if I am a conduit,
it's working.

//

& now it's possible to see where man smolders & smelts

from space, targets like angels' ears,

the oracular keen of a keen

missile's downfall shattering the world one stone at a time

says the earth

I remember when mainstreet was contiguous & so was my family,

the streetlamps like trepanning pins,

the town hall like a spur

says the earth

in a sense all dissolution is atomic, all destruction pits itself against your body's continuity

I could crack any day   *says the earth*
I smell sulfur   *says the earth*

III.

Echo's Diagnosis

the earth can't open its mouth so we are
opening it

(*helpfully*)

dreaming of turning into the rich
dust of our labor

(*piecemeal*)

marching around the country like a jumpsuit
full of dimes

(*shank-shank-shank-stepping*)

when they cut me open
it's an avalanche of change

(*pickup, pickup*)

a doctor says that's what was wrong

Returning to the Sycamore

the sycamore is an atomic cloud but

not like that

you're an atom cloud

everything is

everything is doing its best

the sycamore stabs into the plain & stays there like a good idea

like sunglass safety goggles,

safeties on your guns, or just holding hands

(big leaves around like taken-off

doll dresses)

it's precautionary against dying alone

even if you wake up every morning predicting the rapture

you'll never be right

look at the night peel back from the day

look at my love & tell me it isn't holy

Blood Orange

& you accidentally kiss yourself

in the mirror you made

outside the garden of your window

(beans on coiled nooses, black citrus)

& you accidentally kiss yourself

on the mouth, morning glory

in the morning's thorny glass frost

Blood Orange

I felt that halo

a good long while—

godliness

in the, I think, agnostic sense

pours through me

like a faucet, the upward

hose in spring

wetting the plot.

The prognostication says

Break nothing but bread,

says, *Unbutton all the buttons—*

the sun knifes the trees

then it stitches them back up

Echo's Prognosis

we wish we had more hands so we could make more fists

(*pickup, pickup*)
we wish we had more hands to hold

more coins in
(*more hands is more handfuls*)

the stones are like headless dolls
with excommunicated bodies

reporting (*pickup, pickup*) how
the slagpile plus the ore is the size of the hole

we wish we could box more of everything including ears,
stones like beheaded dolls

with stone-shaped heads

amass in the slagpile,
babes of the town slag-swaddled

everybody thinks he is svelte,

men looking taller & taller
the deeper & deeper the trench is

Assumption Hall

you can hew a staircase   (one going down)

by way of subtraction

or by way of addition (going up) with planks

I regularize our arbors   armed with diminishment

the businesses were bars   the outlier a ministry

I hang from heavens   as though from a steel steeple

atop the duplex   of the mess hall & assumption hall

I don't make anything I make,   I make things proclaim

their thingness (the area above the staircase much like a

staircase)   make a staff of it, a scalar clef of it

in the aural purgatory   between a groundling's *floors*

& the assumption's *stories*   a strata's been broken & so

has a sweat   I recall a love like an overlook

like a striptease of a hillside

it feels like a spree   it might be precondition

only in duress   do we know our bodies   are

Prelude

I am going to start
yelling; I want you to walk away

until I am inaudible
there is no such thing as eye

contact; when we met
you were already onstage

you had amplification even if your
curtains were bedsheets

even if your auditorium was the agnostic basement
of a shithouse

bar, the room so full
it might have been empty

I was like wearing earmuffs
an astronaut fishbowl helmet

I was like
the big bang's videographer

you were singing a song about privilege
primal chaff was burning

in two fields
with you on the fence in between

Song

we were young then   *the country was young*

we had feral nature, territory
expansion plans   *we were young*

still treating our skulls as helmets we didn't
know anybetter   *shithouse earth,*
                                                heart like a dumpster

hadn't seen a bee or a bear in quite some time
not seeing the absent

    forest for the absent trees   *guilt was a migraine*
                                                we didn't have

we had headshots, your dumpster heart unsure
of what it was full of

    like a daisy

I severed myself from earth
to give away to you   *with enough fury,*
                                                ignorance is sustainable

[I will make a space for you]

I will make a space for you

                                      I shot rockets
                                      through a ton of something
                                      to make a ton of absolute nothingness

      smoke cleans
      its sulfuric red paw
      kites like red doves weren't there

                                        flak patterns like paratroopers
                                      lock elbows establish a perimeter

these not-doves
fresh from the armory of thingness—

the trappings of trapping
adorn them

                                      America loves the right
                                      to hollow the tip of anything
                                      or to hollow anything out

valor & value commingle
the crater is like Pompeii but manmade
& not an island & everyone knew

                                      it was a ruin
                                      before the rock bottom shot up

Canopy Fire

we have this in common

    my tiny body hasn't yet grown into its feet or face
    the average American reads no books per year

    the cowshit river's an abysmal
    baptismal, a wineskin looks like a collapsed lung
    but it's really a collapsed stomach

    I believe in Jesus as a hedge

of bets, as a burning box shrub, a tinderbox
as a promise of tenderness
I heard he died in a helicopter—I heard trinities are everywhere

    a three-legged dog & a three-legged man have similar
    conditions but differing problems

I don't know how to count
the phantom limbs I have—I have
    a shorn oak with ringlets & scabs

    the firemen prune trees so they won't burn one another down
    contingencies are weeping all round us
    look at the sky we are dying

    we have this in common

the oak torques under the weight of its phantom crops

we have this in common,
barenecked organs, unsightly bellows

& we have this in common—a tired opacity
& bad falls reddening the water

The Farrier's File

You are my masterwork: a pile of filings.
Like cinnamon strewn.

      Like cinnamon strewn, says a chorus.

From this I could hammer an iron grouse or
a blade to pierce a grouse: potentials
well around a cauldron,

amounting.   *A cauldron, a mounting*, says they.   I wear a riding-hood,

              a fume-hood,
              I wear a nunhood habit

   of rebar bones. I do shavings, I do magnetic
   lines. Trawling a complex tarn, *Did you mean
   you tarnish*, asks they. Ablaze,

a blue oxides.
Your mark is in my workshop.   If you are a soulless horseman
                             I will make you one

      I will make you, threatens a chorus.

Like as a blacksmith smiths, like as a farrier farries. Hammering a night-
mare's stiletto heel

      into the shape of a *you.*

[i am laughing convulsively]

i am laughing convulsively

parts of my hair over the landscape
your reflex is afire

your reflex as fine

as the horse's horseshoe convulsion
dismay was a mirror struck with a mallet

it broke into (n) novembers
and (n-1) decembers

i am laughing about particular matters
i am doing

what all models do
now i may (not) be particular

but i do (not not) matter

Cherry Bomb

The flowers are not blooming
I shepherded bees to the edge of them
Not really of course

Not bees
There are Fords with poise on the edge of the gorge
The kids learn stickshift in them

They learn to clutch
The only true story is my father
Threw a cherry blossom into the backseat of the Mustang

I didn't exist anywhere for decades yet
We were drinking together
The colors themselves were proud

The cherry blossom exploded
The backseat
The upholstery was like a shotgunned cow

I didn't exist anywhere but I wanted to

Assay

a child is born out of labor & into labor
like it wasn't a fall at all
like death is a moot membrane   *after the fashion of life*

    the little chimbleysweeps
    stain your fjords dark black
    like it's so different

                to have a carport
                to live in a carport

                        to live in a car
                        to die in a car

kids stuck on the tracks

                o you're great in the ore-cart,
                you fit into anywhere

    god touches
    his thumb to his forefinger
    like a zero or an okay

                  you could fit thru there

                        pennies on the dollar,
                        lung capacity of an angel

Echo's Halloween

One Halloween I went as the wind, I tied a twine to every
Twig in the thicket, the lesser beasts &

Stones. I put an eyelet of twine around the blooms, your prewar-pre-winter dress.
(It was blue & smelled of dogs,

Twine-entwined.) I say vowels & tighten, the little town contracts
Toward me, low barometer,

Low perimeter, vowel, vowel, thunder, consonant, lightning,
Fistful of threads, the woolen

Dog dress. My adoration has a price, which is your adoration.
I am air-fishing.

The next year
I go as the wind, but I go twineless.

Blood Orange

Blood orange

is a fruit & a quality

of light

I used to climb through

the waxen citrus—

when there were edible orbs

I would pluck

& eat them, when there were

visual blossoms

I beheld them. &

when the boughs went brown

& willowy

in their death throes

I would enact my longevity

amongst them.

Echo's Dreams

Echo dreams of being an Onassis
lookalike, dreams sheer textiles, greenrooms

with checkerboard portents.

//

In the highland umber is a primary color; the others
are olive & marigold.

//

Born with creeds, with bangs, with a cuneiform *how*
hewn in her browline.

Bobbies, bobbins. Plain bobs. One butterfly
harelip. The heavens

hemispheric
to her.

//

She might be bloodless. Dislikes: the garish
parish, the reds, garrisons, quarters

holed up in the amaranth home. The linseed skim
in the crockpot.

//

They say store oil-drums, water-drums, snare-
drums to summon a rain. They say

My body's grotto is sublime
like I am a beige near-vapor.

//

They say a lot of upcountry things thus far upcountry:
Carry a whistle, a frisson. Carry

a lead smock.

If Earth

if earth could heave it would   (I want to know something)
        (no one else knows)

if it could hurl it would   (like *revelations*)

        (a shared unknown in the disguise of)
        (a known)

your mother

        (adjacent)

is reading it

her optimism borders on a deathwish

I want to know if I am a genius, baby   (I need a dumptruck, baby)

we discern glaciers together
Echo & I
they are white horses humping a river of ground

bone
someone
will pawn my heartsleeves, my first editions

I don't care, I want to know something
no one else knows   (the reticent chill)
        (*article, noun, verb*)

reckoning the bony sands
how many grains are left after the bombs'
calculations

I want to sell that number's aftermath
like a line of ocean to the landlocked junkie
the glacier now akin to lace   (shattered)
                                                (the profound needs)
                                                (*article, noun, verb*)

the landlocked superior
a line of junk poem
it's all ribbed, your thinness, it's all atoms   (fault)

the happy is ending   (the profound needs)
                                                (the unprofound fragment)

                                                (the town is a cake)
                                                (of bonemeal in a lake of bonemeal)

I want, I want, I want
man is lurching demands together   (the object subjects; the subject objects)

history is a dumb place to live   (the whole fragments)
                                                (I overlook a mine)

& yet here it is
I don't want a settlement

a roofline that's a billionth of a skyline   (I have no outer space)
                                                (I have no inner god)
                                                (I love my life but hate my lifespan)

man shouldn't make tectonics
man shouldn't *should* on themselves   (crackling knuckles like two knobby logs)

the woven cabin has a billion eyes but it is fine
being legless

                                            (lazy like a lazy eye)

                                            (wandering like a wandering eye)

what if every star had an affiliate *pose*

I think, & then punch my groin   (that one is *kneel covering the back of your neck*)

                                       (there's *interlace with your neighbor*)

what if I don't want one & madness
is in decline
                                       (here is *exponential solitude*)

I think cities existed
long before cities existed   (& the star for *the gesture for shunning* goes out)

Epilogue

[The place I love is burning]

The place I love is burning, the place I love is not burning, none of the places I love are anywhere, a fire so deep in a mine is irrelevant, under the moon everything I love is burning or not burning or *not is*.

The slats are full of the spaces between slats in the place I love the woman I love isn't burning but my love for her is. Her love is full of slats and burning peers through them, a silver column approaches the moon but doesn't even approach the moon.

The moon isn't burning, the place I love is a place a column of steam is, silver departs my sternum, the woman I love is not a place, she isn't anyplace.

Burning isn't burning, I can still feel my hands, I wish she felt anything but at the bottom of the mine is a lonely neuron burning, the place I love is built for testing dark matter, I love it so deeply I have never been there.

The woman I love passes through bowers I love leaving a silver shadow of lossless burning burning a garden. The place I love is that garden.

ACKNOWLEDGMENTS

"Upstate Mothers" and "Assumption Hall" appeared in *Handsome*

"They Found a Wolf" appeared in *Cream City Review*

"Dead Pony Recapitulation" and "The Farrier's File" appeared in *Knock*

"Cherry Bomb" and "Blood Orange" appeared on KAXE's *Beat Poetry*

"[The place I love is burning]" appeared in *Birmingham Poetry Review*

"Dark Sides" appeared in *TriQuarterly Review*

Excerpts from "Anechoic" appeared in *Muse: A Journal*

"Echo's Ailments," "Echo's Impressions," and "Echo's Dreams" appeared in *The Pinch*, and the song "Enough Love / Echo Echo" debuted at *The Pinch* online

Special thanks to my friends and collaborators throughout Minnesota; to the dream team at Milkweed HQ; and to the countless soul-affirming hosts who have welcomed me (and my bandmates and my dog) into their guestrooms, porches, and basements during these last few years on the road. Neither this book, nor this life, would exist without their kindness and support.

//

Brian Laidlaw is a fiscal year 2012 recipient of an Artist Initiative grant from the Minnesota State Arts Board. This activity is made possible in part by a grant from the Minnesota State Arts Board, through an appropriation by the Minnesota State Legislature and by a grant from the National Endowment for the Arts.

LINER NOTES

This book includes a companion album of original music written and performed by the author. Download the *Mirrormaker* LP here:

milkweed.org/the-mirrormaker

[TRACK LISTING]

1. One Little Star (*3:22*)
2. Bull in a China Shop (*4:56*)
3. Sleeping Dogs Lie (*9:58*)
4. These Bones (*2:55*)
5. Enough Love / Echo Echo (*10:25*)
6. Whipping Girl (*6:20*)

[ALBUM CREDITS]

All songs written by Brian Laidlaw
Performed by Brian Laidlaw (*guitar & vocals*), Danny Vitali (*bass & vocals*),
J.T. Bates (*drums*), Jake Hanson (*electric & slide guitar*),
Alex Ramsey (*piano & organ*), Brett Bullion (*auxiliary percussion*),
Greg Byers (*cello*), and Bex Gaunt (*violin*)
Produced by Brett Bullion
Mastered by Huntley Miller
© 2018 by Brian Laidlaw (ASCAP)

Lyrics, news, and tour dates available at www.brianlaidlaw.com

Colin Copp

BRIAN LAIDLAW is a poet-songwriter whose recent releases include the chapbook/LP *Amoratorium*, the 7" vinyl single *Jeremiad*, and the full-length collection *The Stuntman*. He holds an MFA in poetry from the University of Minnesota, and is working toward a PhD in creative writing at the University of Denver. Laidlaw lives in a basement in Boulder, Colorado, and continues to tour nationally and internationally with his band The Family Trade.

Founded as a nonprofit organization in 1980, Milkweed Editions is an independent publisher. Our mission is to identify, nurture and publish transformative literature, and build an engaged community around it.

milkweed.org

Interior design and typesetting by Mary Austin Speaker
Typeset in Bulmer MT

Bulmer is a transitional typeface designed by punchcutter
William Martin in the late eighteenth century to print the Boydell
Shakespeare folio edition. Described as "both delicate and
spirited, thoroughly English" by the typographical historian D. B.
Updike, Bulmer offers higher contrast than its predecessors, and
flourished serifs on the uppercase *R* and *Q*. The digital version of
Bulmer is based upon the foundry version of the typeface, which
was designed by Morris Fuller Benton in 1923
for Monotype Imaging.